DAD: No, you cannot go to the park in the rain. There will be too much mud. Sit down and wait for a bit.
TOM: You can kick there, if it's too wet for you to go out.

Fit to finish

In this book, you will meet:

LIZ   KIT   TOM   DAD

You will need:

Written by Erin Howard
Illustrated by Andrea Bianchi

raintree
a Capstone company — publishers for children

LIZ: Kit and I are off to the park, Dad.
KIT: We need to get better at kicking and shooting.
DAD: The park? But it's raining out there.
LIZ: Can we go in the rain if we have coats?

LIZ: Can we, Dad?
DAD: Yes, that's all right by me, if you are good!
KIT: Thanks, we will not get under your feet! Let's go, Liz!
TOM: Wait for me. I will get this box for you.

TOM: Your turn now, Kit. Back up and aim for the box.
KIT (kicking): I missed, but it was near.
LIZ: I think your kick was a bit too hard.
KIT: Yes, I think so, too. Off you go, Liz, good luck.

LIZ (kicking): Can I keep kicking until I get it in the box?
KIT: Wow, it's in! No need to keep going.
TOM: Good job, Liz.
KIT: Look at you hopping up and down!

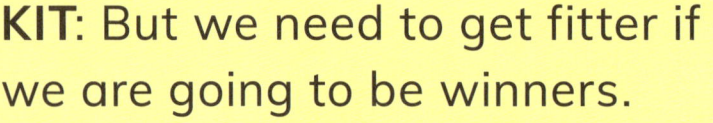

KIT: But we need to get fitter if we are going to be winners.
LIZ: Yes, if we are not fit, we will not finish.
KIT: And if we do not finish, we cannot win. We have to be fit to finish!
LIZ: Then let's keep going.
TOM: Can you do tap-the-top? Tap the top with this foot. Then, tap the top with that foot. This foot, then that foot, and so on. But do not kick it!

KIT: If you can do it, Coach Tom, we can, too! Yes, I'm doing it!
LIZ: Tap, tap. Oh no! I kicked it. Sit right there, you!
KIT: It is not a dog, Liz. It will not do as you tell it!
LIZ: Tap-the-top seems hard.

TOM: Let's do the bell tap, then. To do the bell tap, you tap with this foot to that foot, then back with that foot to this foot. You tap with the arch of your foot.
KIT: Is that all, Tom? I think I can do the bell tap.
LIZ: I do not think I can do it.

KIT: I will have a go. Tap with this foot. Then tap with that foot. Oh, I cannot do it!

LIZ: Nor can I. Tom, can the box go up high, so I can shoot hoops?

DAD (yelling): I can hear you, Liz! No shooting hoops!

LIZ: I'm hot. I think I will sit for a bit.
KIT: Oh, I cannot do a bell tap! Do not tell Tom!
LIZ: He's back! I did the bell tap, Tom.
KIT: And so did I.
TOM: I do not think you did it at all!

KIT: You are right, Tom. I did not do it, but I am fitter.

TOM: That's good. If you are fit, you will finish. And if you finish, you can win.

KIT: I will kick and run and hop and tap and shoot. I am fit to finish, you will see!

LIZ: I will go with you. But I will sit in the sun. I am fit to finish right now, too. I am fit to finish ... my book!